Ciara's Gift

To Kathleen & Sean

Mrs Glennon

Ciara's Gift

Grief edged with gold

UNA GLENNON

UWA PUBLISHING

To all parents who have lost a child.
Grieving never ends but it does not end life.

What is your life?
You are a mist that appears for a little while
and then vanishes.

James 4:14

THIS BOOK WAS BORN OUT of my grief journey following the murder of our daughter Ciara. It is a book I never would have wished to write but it has become the book I must write, for not to do so would seem unfaithful. It is my story, but it could also be the story of every parent who has lost a child.

It is taken from jottings I wrote down at the time, interspersed with my vivid memories of events, and is comprised of short, self-contained segments. A grieving person may open the book at any segment, read it and identify with it or use it for further reflection. I have attempted to show some sequence through which my journey took me, but if I have not always succeeded it is because there is no sequence to grief. If my memories of events differ from those of others, please forgive me. I have attempted to be as truthful and as accurate as my experiences and recollections allow.

This is a story of love, despair, searching, spiritual awakening, acceptance and finally peace. During my struggle to come to terms with Ciara's death, books were very important to me. They provided me with metaphors and images that helped me to understand and express my grief. They also gave me the means with which to probe the mystery of life and death. It is my wish that my book may provide similar consolation to those who are at present journeying through grief. It is possible to survive the worst of all tragedies and to emerge a fuller, stronger and better human being as a result.

My experience compelled me to write this book but there was always a second motivation. I believe that this book allows something else of lasting value to emerge from Ciara's life and the tragedy of her death.

This book is Ciara's gift to you.

Each age is a dream that is dying
Or one that is coming to birth.

ARTHUR O'SHAUGHNESSY

THE DRONE OF THE VC 8 pierces the silence as I slowly emerge from a restless, comfortless sleep. Awareness dawns as my eyes become accustomed to the muted light in the aircraft cabin and the crumpled, sleeping passengers emerge into view.

I stretch my aching body and quietly raise the shutter on the aircraft window. The unveiling of a new day has just begun. The black night sky is fringed with a band of deep red along the horizon. Gradually the band dissolves into varying shades of pink and mauve as it extends further into the sky and the inky darkness fades into a dull grey. As the pinks and mauves begin to fade, without warning a great ball of gold bursts over the horizon, revealing in all their beauty and mystery the sweeping sands of the Sahara desert below. I hold my breath as if to halt time, the drama of the event reaching deep inside, making me profoundly aware that I have just experienced something majestic, almost mystical. A new day is born. It is not just any new day. It is also the birthing of a new life for me. My husband of two weeks and I are on our way to start our married life in Zambia, Central Africa.

I am filled with excitement and anticipation for our new life ahead. But deep down there is also the awareness of what I am leaving behind in Ireland. I am leaving behind my family and friends whom I love dearly and all the people who supported and nurtured me. I am leaving behind my culture and everything that made me who I am. I am leaving behind the name I was known by for the last twenty-three years. From now on I will be known only by my married name. I am leaving behind part of my very identity.

It is 1968 and air travel is not so easy or common. I will not return to Ireland for at least two-and-a-half years.

I am learning one of the great lessons in life. With every new beginning there has to be an ending.

I HAVE SETTLED INTO LIFE in Zambia. Shortly after our arrival we experience a water shortage. All the students in the Teacher Training College where I am lecturing are sent home to their villages and towns until the rainy season begins. We watch our water supply dwindle until only a brown murky liquid trickles from our taps. It is evident that we must also leave. As we receive only a modest stipend from the mission where we are working, our financial resources are limited. We buy an old Peugeot 304 car and a tent, and head south into Rhodesia (now Zimbabwe).

We are fortunate to have time on our side as we meander through the countryside, pitching our tent wherever we choose. Here, unspoiled by human interference, nature displays herself in all her splendour. Each day is filled with wonder and reverence, a feast for our senses and our souls. Sleeping with only a piece of canvas between us and the stars, we are immersed in the sounds and smells of nature. Here, humans and animals live a respectful co-existence. It is not unusual to have to stop to allow a herd of elephants to cross the road, or to be awakened by the sound of some wild animal chomping outside our tent or the early morning screeches of monkeys high in the trees above.

Here, there is time and space for reflection, for interiority. From the vastness of the night skies viewed from the stillness and isolation of the Matopos Hills, the chosen burial place of Cecil Rhodes, to the smallest of living creatures crawling in the bare earth around our tent, I am constantly reminded of the mystery and magnificence of the universe. Briefly I ponder the vast web of life and humankind's place and purpose in it all. But it is only a brief contemplation, for the exuberance of youth still courses through my veins, urging me on to new experiences, to greater adventures.

Sorrow had not yet dimmed my vision or slowed me in my tracks.

IT IS HOLIDAY TIME AGAIN at the college. This time we plan to travel north-east into Tanzania, our destination being Dar es Salaam on the east coast and returning to Zambia through Malawi, an epic trip of some five thousand kilometres. As Zambia is a landlocked country and the government has imposed sanctions against Rhodesia, all imported goods must be transported by road from the port of Dar es Salaam. This busy road is nothing more than a corrugated dirt track and very potholed. It is not called the 'Hell Run' for nothing. We take off in our sturdy Peugeot with nothing more than two spare wheels, a jerry can with extra petrol, our two-person tent, canned and dried food and a Michelin map covering the entire continent of Africa.

As we travel north I am struck by the remoteness of the region, the absence of towns and the scarcity of people. The landscape is largely uninteresting and inhospitable, mainly low scrub. There is not the same sense of freedom and safety I encountered in Rhodesia. We only use our tent when absolutely necessary. There is an unspoken code of hospitality among the missionaries and there is always an open door for weary travellers. We sleep in a leprosarium one night, on another night in a dusty unused monk's cell on an isolated mission station.

As we enter Tanzania the landscape changes. Each day brings new visual delights. The road meanders through lush forests, past native villages of thatched mud huts, along steep escarpments, and we catch our first sight of wildlife. The distances between towns are not so great here and we can pace our trip so we are in a town each night.

Almost from the moment we leave I am feeling nauseous. It soon becomes evident it is not just carsickness. I am pregnant. The trip takes on a new perspective. My awareness shifts from the miracle of nature without to the miracle of life that is taking place within.

We finally reach Dar es Salam with its azure sea and palm-fringed white powdery beaches. This is a city that engages the senses. Sights, sounds and smells reflect the rich diversity of cultures the city embraces. Our time here is brief but enjoyable.

Our return trip through Malawi brings us again into very isolated landscapes. Apart from my almost continual nausea, our days are carefree. The countryside is beautiful. We camp by the shores of Lake Malawi and completely lose track of the days of the week. The people we encounter speak very little English and do not have the same concern for knowing what day it is. Not to be aware of or constrained by time gives a whole new meaning to freedom.

But we are still bound by the calendar and must keep moving. As we leave Malawi we are stopped by the Malawi Youth—an army of young men who patrol the country. They retain us for an inordinate length of time, searching our car and taking out all our belongings. They are like children, full of curiosity about the items they find in our luggage. I am decidedly uncomfortable with these youths as they skittishly play with our possessions and their loaded guns. Relief comes when they eventually allow us to repack our car and move on. Our wonderful holiday has been marred by the actions of these young men, drunk with power and authority.

All I want now is to return to Zambia to allow our baby to grow and develop in the safety of our own home.

You know your life has changed forever,
For in all the days and years to come,
Distance will never be able to cut you off
From the one you now carry
For nine months under your heart.

JOHN O'DONOHUE

I AM SITTING IN THE back row of the college hall watching a movie, some B-grade action-packed production, with the student body. The students really love these movies. They whistle and cheer-on the good guys and hoot and boo at the bad guys. Every so often a reel has to be changed or the projector breaks down and the students impatiently hiss and whistle until the projector spurts into life again and the movie resumes. I am here not out of interest but in a supervisory capacity and tonight my husband is operating the projector. My mind drifts into reverie. I am vaguely aware of the clickitty-clack of the projector in the background, the swirls of dust particles in the shaft of light coming from the small square hole in the projection room wall, the flickering on the screen, then suddenly, a faint fluttering inside me. There it goes again, like the movement of a bubble, the flick of a feather. It is not a familiar feeling.

I hold my breath in wonder as it suddenly dawns on me: this is my baby's first movement.

The significance of the event fills me with excitement and awe. I long to share my secret but there is no one near, just the students around me fully engrossed in what is taking place on the screen, totally oblivious to the miracle that has just occurred in their midst. For me it is a momentous occasion, one I will carry with me for the rest of my life. Miracles are continually taking place in the deep and dark recesses of our lives and most of the time we are so taken up with the busyness of life that they happen without us even noticing.

I ENJOY PREPARING FOR OUR new baby. Our nearest store, owned by an Indian trader, is about ten kilometres away. It stocks almost everything from sewing needles to bags of maize to engine oil. Although it doesn't stock baby items or maternity wear it does have a good supply of materials, so I set to and make maternity dresses, baby rugs and wraps. But there are many items we cannot purchase, so we head off again to Rhodesia (Zimbabwe) during our next holidays.

I am heavily pregnant so we stay in a hotel and concentrate on rest and relaxation and purchasing the necessities for our baby. I buy nappies and baby clothes, wool, patterns, crochet hooks and knitting needles. I am going to enjoy knitting and crocheting items for our baby and it will help to fill in my leisure time while waiting for the birth. Lastly, we buy a pram.

I am happy with my simple purchases as we set off on our return journey but we still have the hurdle of crossing the border. Having come from a border town in Ireland, I have a necessary respect for and indeed fear of border crossings. This time is no different. The customs officials unpack our entire luggage and under some obscure, implausible pretext, confiscate all the baby items. One does not try to reason or argue with customs officials. We return to our home with only the pram, knitting needles and patterns. Africans have no use for these items.

MY PREGNANCY PROGRESSES NORMALLY AND soon it is November. The rains are late. As the days pass the heat builds up, forming a shimmering haze over the landscape. There is no relief. All of nature languishes in the heat. The soil is parched and powdery. Insect eggs and seeds lie dormant underneath, waiting for the first drops of rain that will stir them into life. Dogs lie panting in the scanty shade. Life is suspended, waiting for the impending rain. With each passing day our senses become more heightened as we listen for the distant rumblings of thunder or scan the horizon for the buildup of storm clouds that announce the first downpour. We sniff the air in the hope of detecting that welcome earthy aroma of the first few drops. A sense of expectation looms as people become more lethargic in the oppressive heat.

I am also full of expectation as I await the arrival of our baby. Will it be a boy or a girl? If it is a girl we will call her Ciara. The baby is in the breech position and showing no signs of turning. If it doesn't turn soon I will have an early caesarean section. I continue to lecture each day as I await the decision. I have no apprehension about what lies ahead of me. I have total faith in the young Irish doctor who is also a nun and who will deliver my baby in the small mission hospital that services this area.

THE HOSPITAL IS RUN BY five Irish nuns—four nurses and one doctor. It is a sixty kilometre drive over a dusty, corrugated road. There are no other medical personnel in the area and the hospital is very understaffed. The local people really depend on this facility and it is kept very busy. It consists mainly of two large wards, one for males and one for females, and both are always overflowing. Extra mattresses are shoved in between the beds to accommodate the extra patients. When women are admitted they invariably bring their babies and toddlers. Food is not provided. Instead families arrive with their charcoal stoves and cook maize porridge, the staple food and the only meal of the day. If the patient is well enough she cooks her own meals.

All this activity takes place in the central quadrangle of the hospital. Many of the patients are women who have come to give birth, others are suffering from malaria or dysentery and many of them carry tuberculosis.

Into this setting Ciara enters the world by caesarian section on the twentieth of November 1969, ten days before she is due. She is delivered at 6:30am before the heat of the day builds up and conditions become too uncomfortable in the basic theatre. The young doctor who performs the operation also administers the anaesthetic and is assisted by a single nurse. Some hours later when the effect of the general anaesthetic has worn off, I am presented with my baby. She is a perfect baby, a perfect example of the miracle of life. She is also the first newborn baby I have ever held.

As SOON AS POSSIBLE I struggle out of bed and make my way to the nursery where Ciara is kept. As I enter, I sense there is someone behind the door. I turn to look and am momentarily transfixed. Sitting on the floor is a woman feeding her baby. Her body is frail and ravaged by leprosy. Her dull and wrinkled skin hangs from her skeletal frame. She wears only a shabby chetenga (sarong) tied around her waist. Her extremities are missing, eroded by her cruel disease. She holds her baby to her obviously empty, pendulous breast with fingerless hands. Her baby is tiny, barely clinging to life. She looks up and our eyes lock momentarily. Her life of suffering is visible in her deep sad eyes. In that brief moment of encounter something deep inside me is touched and I too feel the burden of her suffering.

I turn away clumsily, confused and unsettled. I am too shocked to speak, she too humble.

Later I speak with the nurse. She assures me that the disease is arrested, that my baby is not in jeopardy, but she also tells me this same woman comes into the hospital each year to give birth and each year she goes home alone. Her babies never survive.

I am deeply affected by the plight of this mother, by the contrast between her life and mine: between our birth experiences, between our babies' life expectancies. I return to my home with a heart full of joy at the new addition to our family, but at the same time carrying a deep feeling for all the mothers whose birth experience is not as happy as mine. Joy and sorrow live side by side.

Nothing could have prepared your heart
to open like this.

JOHN O'DONOHUE

BACK HOME WITH OUR NEW baby, the real meaning of unconditional love begins to unfold. No task is too great or sacrifice too much for the welfare of this new life we have brought into the world and for which we are now totally responsible. Living on a mission station with only nuns and priests for company, I have no one to turn to for advice about babies. I am totally on my own. On one of his rare trips to the capital Lusaka, my husband buys Dr. Spock's book on child care. It becomes my bible. At times the responsibility of motherhood is overwhelming but I am rewarded a hundred fold by the increasing bond of trust and love that grows with each passing week.

Life had changed for us now; no more wandering through the untamed parts of Africa. The priority now is the health and welfare of our baby.

Fifteen months later we are joined by Ciara's sister, Denise, and our family is complete. They are both happy children who bring great joy and love into our lives. As we live in an isolated community away from extended family, our small nuclear family becomes very close-knit. Ciara and Denise become inseparable. We have none of the trappings of modern day society. There is no television and only a limited supply of toys, and lollies are almost unheard of. But the children have a freedom and an exposure to the natural world that they would not have in a modern city. We continue to travel frequently, back to Ireland and Europe during our long holidays and throughout the southern parts of Africa in our short breaks.

All too quickly the years pass and it is time for Ciara to start school and we decide it is also time for us to put down some roots. Chasing the sun we decide to move to Perth, Western Australia.

We soon settle into life in Perth.

As Ciara grows and develops it becomes evident that she is blessed with many gifts. She has a cheerful, friendly disposition. She acquires a wide circle of good friends and is herself a loyal friend. She is totally honest and open in her relationships. She has a good intellect and a talent for any sport she chooses to play. She represents her school in swimming and athletics, and on the debating and public speaking teams. She takes part in her school's drama and musical productions. She demonstrates a quiet determination to succeed at everything she attempts and will not let anything beat her. Yet, she is not competitive and takes delight in the achievements of her friends. Ballet becomes a major part of her life and here she also shows great potential. But when it comes to choosing a career she decides on the legal profession.

After her first year at university, Ciara is one of a small group offered the opportunity to study two degrees simultaneously. Relishing another challenge, she embarks on a demanding study programme for both Law and Arts degrees, the latter with majors in Industrial Relations and Japanese. During these years Ciara studies diligently but also enjoys a good social life. Her open, friendly and vivacious personality immediately puts people at ease. By the sheer warmth of her presence she can light up a room. She is natural and unassuming: what you see is how she is and she says exactly what she thinks.

The years pass swiftly and all too soon our two girls finish university and embark on their respective careers. Ciara takes up a position with a large law firm in Perth and the following year is admitted to the Bar. Denise has qualified in Medicine. I feel life is complete. We have launched our children successfully on the stage of life. Now it is time for my husband and me.

These are happy times. We have not yet discovered the meaning of the word grief.

AFTER FOUR BUSY YEARS WORKING in the legal profession, Ciara decides to take a year off to travel. During her year overseas I take an armchair journey with her. Some of the places she visits I have not even heard of: the islands of Nias in Indonesia and Kho Samui in Thailand and Elat in Israel are all unknown to me, so the first thing I do is find them on a map, then if possible, get a video and immerse myself in the scenery and the culture she is experiencing. I visit these places through her eyes. She phones regularly and this becomes another way of journeying with her. She travels extensively through Israel, Turkey and Greece. She crosses Europe and spends some months with relatives in Ireland.

I am really pleased that she is having this wonderful experience but I am apprehensive for her safety. I know I will be more settled when she returns to Perth.

She finally arrives home via the U.S.A. on the first of March looking relaxed, rested and happy, and I breathe a sigh of relief. After a week of readjustment and catching up with friends, she returns to her very busy working life.

Joy and sorrow are inseparable:
together they come and when one sits alone with you,
remember that the other is asleep under your bed.

Kahlil Gibran

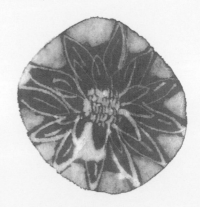

FRIDAY THE FOURTEENTH OF MARCH dawns. It is just another ordinary day, no premonitions, no foreboding of what is about to happen. I have a busy day planned.

The law firm where Ciara is employed is having drinks after work to celebrate St. Patrick's Day. Ciara plans to attend and then have an early night. I drive her to the bus stop in the morning. She sold her car before going overseas and has not yet had the time to replace it. I offer to pick her up later but she declines. She will get a lift home with a friend or catch a taxi. We say a hasty goodbye and she says 'thanks Mum' as she gets out of the car. I speak to her again at five o'clock. Her plans have not altered. She says she is tired. I suggest she doesn't attend the drinks after work, but she says she thinks she should.

That is the last time I speak with her.

It is now Saturday morning and Ciara did not return home last night. This has never happened before. Something untoward must have happened. I must not panic. There is probably a perfectly good explanation. It is now 1pm and still no sign of Ciara. I have spoken with her friends and found out that she and two work colleagues got a lift with one of the partners in their law firm. He dropped them off at the Continental Hotel in Claremont, close to where he lives and just ten minutes from our home. There she chatted with some friends but she was in a hurry to get home. She didn't even take the time to have a drink but left after about twenty minutes to catch a taxi home. Her two colleagues stayed on.

Fear is beginning to take hold and I ring the police. Very soon a young police officer arrives. I am now very worried. As the officer laboriously writes down my answers to his questions, I am silently screaming at him to hurry up and get a search party out to look for Ciara. But there is a process that has to be adhered to and I will have to be patient. I remain calm outwardly, with no hint of the terror that is welling up inside.

By late evening when Ciara fails to keep a dinner engagement, the police finally accept that she is missing, and the nightmare begins.

THE DAYS FOLLOWING CIARA'S DISAPPEARANCE are filled with shock, confusion and turmoil. I stumble from moment to moment in a daze, not knowing what to do or where to turn. I cannot think. My mind is numb. When I am asked a question I have to repeat the question in my mind before it registers. Then it is an effort to gather my thoughts to reply. I feel strangely disconnected with everything that is unfolding around me, as if I am on the sideline looking in. My body is tense with pain. It is a searing physical ache as if every nerve ending is exposed and it stretches from the very core of my being to the tips of my fingers and toes. My heart is in a continual spasm of pain.

I can perform only perfunctory tasks. I pace the house, make tea, answer the phone and greet the flow of people who come to offer their support. But all the time I am waiting for that one phone call to tell me Ciara has been found.

It is Monday evening, three days since Ciara's disappearance. It has been another day of agonizing turmoil. I have informed my family in Ireland but my husband has decided not to telephone his elderly parents, also living in Ireland. He still expects Ciara to walk in at any moment.

I answer the phone. It is a journalist from an Irish newspaper. I naively plead with him to hold the story until my husband informs his parents. I explain to him that they are elderly, that his eighty-three-year old mother has just undergone heart surgery, that we need just a few more hours to find a way to break the news to them. He is totally unmoved. His reply will be etched in my memory forever. 'This is a good story,' he says. 'A good story cannot be delayed.'

I beg and plead with him to give us just a few hours but he remains unmoved.

This is my first encounter with journalists or the media. The Australian press has so far been considerate and unobtrusive, so this comes as another unexpected, cruel blow. I realise that this, too, must be dealt with.

We will have to brace ourselves for the onslaught of the media.

THE POLICE COMMISSIONER HAS REQUESTED a meeting with us. We arrive at the Police Headquarters and are ushered through winding corridors to a meeting room. It is a large stark room decorated in varying shades of brown with no adornment. Immediately my eyes are drawn to a large poster of Ciara lying on the coffee table. It is the first time I have seen this poster; I didn't even know it existed. As we wait, sitting on the brown leather seats around the coffee table, the beautiful, plaintive eyes of my daughter stare out at me. It is too much. My husband picks up the poster and removes it out of sight.

The Commissioner arrives. He assures us the police are doing their utmost to find Ciara. It is just prior to the long Easter weekend. The police are advertising widely that there will be extra police presence on the roads in an effort to prevent traffic accidents. I ask the Commissioner if the extra police could be deployed to search for Ciara instead. He replies, 'There will be many mothers in Perth who will be grateful for the extra police presence on the roads over the weekend.' I feel diminished, ashamed that I asked the question. The Commissioner appears very uncomfortable. He fidgets and keeps looking at his watch. The conversation is stilted and soon the meeting disintegrates. I leave feeling we were simply a burden and puzzled about the purpose of the meeting.

EASTER SATURDAY—WE RECEIVE THE first rain of the season and there is a notable chill in the air. It is an appropriately sombre day. The air is filled with a grey curtain of rain. I feel restless, confused and helpless. I pace the house in silence. I feel so fragile. I walk slowly, delicately, tentatively placing my foot on the floor so as not to disturb the cool air around me. Any sudden movement, any jolt, any loud noise would surely shatter me into a thousand pieces and I would float slowly, silently, to the floor in a pile of dust.

I gaze out the window at the misty rain. Is it rain or my tear-filled eyes? I feel the cold of the air on my skin and shiver.

Where are you Ciara? Are you cold, or has your captor, in a moment of kindness, allowed you to wear your jacket?

EASTER SUNDAY, I ATTEND MASS in the local convent. TV crews have been turning up at Sunday Mass in our local church so I am glad of the privacy this chapel offers me. Here I can cry silently, openly, away from the prying cameras. I am still tense with shock and the pain continues to rack my body with the ferocity of physical suffering. I sit in the chapel silently crying, unable to pray, unable to think.

Suddenly an overwhelming calmness overcomes me. It starts at the core of my being and spreads outwards until I am completely enveloped in it and the acute physical pain dissipates.

I somehow know that Ciara is no longer suffering, that she is no longer on this earth.

I am aware that something beyond my control or understanding has just taken place and I accept it without question.

The sense of disconnectedness I have felt since Ciara's disappearance now gives way to a sense of disbelief, a sense of powerlessness.

IT IS NOW ALMOST THREE weeks since Ciara's disappearance. Three weeks of frenzied, agonizing activity. The police are in constant contact. My husband and I both make a television appeal for information. Various organisations and church groups hold prayer services for Ciara's safe return and we are invited to all of them. Our phones ring constantly. Friends and total strangers phone to offer their support. Their kindness is in sharp contrast to the cruelty of the event.

There are many phone calls from people who think they may have information.

Every phone call is important. Every phone call must be taken, in case it provides that one piece of information that would lead us to Ciara.

*When you were young you put on
your own belt and walked where you liked,
but when you grow old you will stretch out
your hand and somebody will put a belt around you
and take you where you would rather not go.*

John 21:18

EARLY ON THE THURSDAY MORNING builders arrive at the house next door to erect a pergola, just across the wall from our indoor and outdoor living areas. Their cheerfulness and activity is a painful contrast to my anguish and inertia. Around eleven o'clock my husband phones. A body has been found. The police are in transit to the location. They are anxious to inform us as the media have intercepted the police radio communication and are also rushing to the location. It will be on the airwaves soon. The police don't want us to hear it first through the media. A formal identification will have to be made.

The wait that follows is excruciating. The police never communicate with me directly. Information is conveyed through my husband so there is no opportunity to get direct answers to my questions. This adds to my feelings of helplessness and isolation. Very soon television crews take up position directly opposite our house, determined to obtain some footage in order to spill our grief into every lounge room in Australia on the evening news.

The inner turmoil, the lack of contact with the police, the incessant, repetitive sound of the nail gun and the builders' cheerful voices next door, the inability to escape, to even go for a walk because of the TV cameras, all merge together to create a living hell.

I know now that hell is here on earth.

By late afternoon I receive confirmation that it is Ciara's body.

Later in the evening I answer the phone. A low haunting voice slowly utters the word 'dead' and then there is silence. Fear grips me as I feel the hair on the back of my neck slowly rise and a chill runs through my body. Later the police trace the call to a fourteen-year-old boy.

About suffering they were never wrong,
The old masters: how well they understood
Its human position; how it takes place
While someone else is eating or opening
a window or just walking dully along.

W. H. Auden

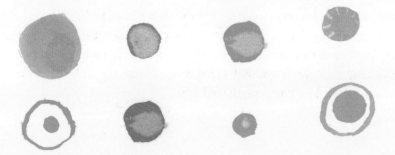

WE NOW MUST TURN OUR attention to planning the funeral. We must give Ciara a befitting farewell, one that will honour her life. But how can you put your heart into something you never ever wanted to have to do?

Friends and people we have never met before rally round. Their support and generosity are boundless. They never intrude but are always on hand to provide whatever help we require. They alleviate the burden of this terrible time more than they will ever know.

We must choose a burial plot in the local cemetery. As I sit waiting in the reception area of the cemetery I am totally bewildered by the normality of everything that is going on around me: people going about their everyday business. Don't they know what has happened? Don't they know that these are not normal times? Scattered on the coffee table are some women's magazines with their banal headlines and pictures. They seem so out of place in this setting, where life should be honoured and respected, not trivialised and sullied in this way.

We finally choose a plot for Ciara in the new lawn area, a plot facing west, facing the setting sun, the sea and the beach, which she loved.

Later we visit the funeral home. It is a sterile place. The day is hot and I have difficulty breathing. I long for a glass of water but am unable to ask for one and none is offered. The attendant is respectful, efficient. Business-like. We are shown a folder containing different styles of caskets and we must choose one. It is difficult to remain focused. Do we want white or black cars, male or female attendees?

What does it matter! I don't want any of this.

I just want Ciara back and life to return to what it was.

Finally the police release Ciara's body and we can set a date for the funeral.

Requiescat

Tread lightly she is near
Under the snow,
Speak gently, she can hear
The daisies grow.

All her bright golden hair
Tarnished with rust,
She that was young and fair
Fallen to dust.

Lily-like, white as snow,
She hardly knew
She was a woman, so
Sweetly she grew.

Coffin-board, heavy stone,
Lie on her breast,
I vex my heart alone,
She is at rest.

Peace, Peace, she cannot hear
Lyre or sonnet,
All my life's buried here,
Heap earth upon it.

OSCAR WILDE

I PIN THIS POEM IN a prominent place. The words somehow give expression to my thoughts and feelings in a way that I cannot. My life is over. My life is buried with Ciara. Only my physical presence remains. The future stretches out before me, a future without Ciara: empty, meaningless.

How can I go on living when there is nothing to live for? I simply have to go through the motions.

I will never smile again.

There will never again be any joy in my life.

Life will be nothing more than a pretence from now until death finally brings release.

THE FUNERAL IS OVER. CIARA's short life has been dutifully wrapped up, sealed and ceremoniously dispatched. People return to the routine of their lives but I am still dazed, reeling in shock. Like a person whose immune system has collapsed, I am completely vulnerable. I have lost the ability to think, to judge, to decide, to act and I am at the whim of every suggestion. I am a robot stumbling around in a maze.

It is important to be surrounded by good friends at this time, friends who have our welfare at heart. One such friend insists that we go and stay in his holiday house for a few days. We do his bidding. It is the right thing to do. Here, we can be alone in our sadness, away from the phones, the police, the media, the chaos. The house is situated among trees with the beach and the ocean just metres away at the end of the bush garden. It is a place of tranquillity, a place to attempt to make sense of what happened, to attempt to begin the long journey back to the land of the living.

The time is passed almost totally in stunned silence. Any conversation revolves around our total disbelief. We read about grief, we walk, we swim. I watch the tears fall from the eyes of my remaining daughter, enormous tears that fall like raindrops onto a cushion she is cradling in her lap. Each tear forms a damp circle that expands further and further outwards as the fabric absorbs the warm moisture. I didn't know that tears could be so big. My body is racked with inner sobs for the pain that she is suffering and for my inability to console.

Where is my husband, the man I married, the man with the twinkling Irish eyes, the man who could lighten any conversation or diffuse any situation with his clever use of words and his ready wit? He is gone now. He has lost the spring from his step and the light from his eyes. Only a lifeless shell remains.

We have become the walking dead.

Despair weakens our sight and closes our ears.
We can see nothing but spectres of doom and
can hear only the beating of our agitated heart.

KAHLIL GIBRAN

WE RETURN HOME AFTER OUR time away and Denis has to return to work. I am alone for the first time since the funeral. I decide to go for a walk. As I step onto the roadway I am suddenly paralysed. My feelings of total desolation and confusion cannot be reconciled to the scene of ordinariness and calm I encounter, and my body rebels. I cannot take one more step forward and make a hasty retreat to the security of my home.

Sometime later I decide to go shopping. In the supermarket I am suddenly gripped by what I later realise is a panic attack and I have to rush from the store. The normality of everything around me is too life-affirming. I have become a stranger in this world. I am enveloped in a haze of sadness. I see everything through a veiled dimness as if someone had reached out and turned down the light. Colours have lost their intensity. Voices and the sounds of nature are hollow and distant. Music, radio and television are unwelcome intrusions. I know that life still goes on but I am not tuned into it. I am operating on a different frequency.

With each passing day the house becomes more and more silent as Ciara's death drains the life from it and I am drawn further and further into my world of darkness. The torpor of grief takes over. I have no interest in anything. There are no meals prepared; bills are left unopened and unpaid; dust begins to pile up. Things that were once considered important now have little meaning.

We are born. We die. These are the only significant events. Everything else is of no consequence.

I LIVE IN AN IN-BETWEEN world. My physical being is here but my mind, my essence, is in another realm. It wanders in some unknown realm between life and death, a place of murky, viscous darkness where everything is dim and distant and where every thought and movement is laboured. The only thing I am aware of is that Ciara is dead, that she will never be coming home again.

I long to catch a glimpse of her, to see where she is now and to know that she is safe, but the barrier between us is dark and impenetrable.

So I wander aimlessly in this miasma, unable to lift myself out of it.

FRIENDS CONTINUE TO BE SUPPORTIVE. Many continue to include us in their social lives but I am incapable of joining in. Ciara's death is the prism through which I see and interpret everything now. I want to talk about her but the subject stops conversation, so I learn to remain silent. The effort required to socialise is exhausting. I can only cope with people for short periods of time. Then I rush home to be alone.

Other friends visit. Their desire to help is etched on their faces but they don't know how to and I cannot tell them. They don't even know what to say. But there is nothing to say. We know what happened and this becomes our silent exchange. There is communion in the silence, as heart weeps with heart.

Touch is now a comforting language. So much is conveyed in a silent embrace. I sense and feel the empathy, the compassion, the connection; I need this and I draw strength from it. Letters and cards of sympathy flood in and I read each one carefully. I am deeply moved that so many people are touched by the tragedy of Ciara's death. I glean great comfort from their words of sympathy and encouragement, from the stories of sorrow they share and from the fact that so many people have taken the time to make contact. Reading the letters lifts me temporarily out of my dark place and connects me with people in a way I can cope with.

I wonder how I will ever be able to reply to all these letters so I pack them away to be dealt with at a later date. Maybe when I am stronger.

Other friends seem to cope with the situation by avoiding me. I watch as the parents of a very good school friend of Ciara's duck and weave in the supermarket to avoid meeting me. Others suddenly cross the street when they see me.

At first I am puzzled by this but then I realise that this is their way of coping and I accept that.

We all cope differently and this too is to be respected.

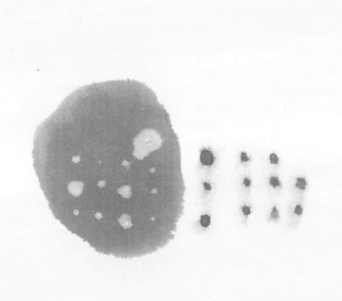

I AM GRIPPED BY FEAR, trapped within its confines. I fear for my own safety and for that of my family. If someone can disappear from a busy highway, how much more vulnerable are we in our own homes? I lock all the windows and doors. I try to imagine and relive the terror Ciara would have felt before she died, as if by reliving it I could somehow take some of it from her.

I fear death.

I cannot even verbalise the word 'dead', much less associate death with Ciara. Day after day I sit and force myself to repeat over and over again in my mind the words 'dead, Ciara is dead'. I breathe the words in, allowing them to spread out and permeate my whole being until the reality begins to set in that Ciara is indeed dead and we will never see her again on this earth.

But what follows death? Where is Ciara now? Where is God in all this? My Christian upbringing taught me that God is a loving God but a loving God would not have allowed this to happen.

The very foundation of everything I believed in is shattered and I am left terrified, stranded on a precipice with nothing to hold on to.

I believed that our souls are immortal, that death is not the end, that we move on to spend the rest of eternity with God. What does all that mean? Blind faith does not suffice any more.

I have to find out for myself. My very survival depends on this.

I need to know where Ciara is now, or whether death is the end.

Learning nourishes the seed,
but it gives you no seed of your own.

KAHLIL GIBRAN

READING HAS NOW BECOME MY lifeline. All my certainties about God and eternal life have been reduced to ashes and I must start from the very beginning. My need to know if life continues beyond death is paramount. I need to know where Ciara is now and what she is experiencing. My very survival centres on the existence or otherwise of what I call God.

Where better to start than at the beginning of time. I need to ensure that my thinking is in no way compromised by my Catholic upbringing, so the first book I read is Stephen Hawking's *A Brief History of Time*. Here is an eminent physicist, acclaimed academic and declared agnostic; surely this book will dismantle once and for all my traditional religious beliefs and start me on a more intellectual, knowledge-based road of understanding and perhaps, freedom.

Day after day, I sit with my books piled high beside me. I am there when Denis leaves for work in the morning and I am still there when he returns home in the evening. I continue until exhaustion forces me to retire to bed at night. I only leave the house to find some more books or to seek out and talk with someone who I think may be able to help me in my quest. I move from physics to metaphysics to quantum physics, from philosophy to theology. I am driven by a feverish and frustrated energy because the more I read the more I realise that we do not know. Eventually I realise that no amount of academic reading is going to provide answers to my questions.

I move to books that explore spirituality. I cast my net wide and draw from all belief systems, ancient and modern, religious and culturally-based. I read the works of shamans and prophets, wisdom writers and mystics. It is all very interesting but I am not reading out of interest. I am seeking understanding. I am reading for my survival.

Gradually I come to the realisation that my quest is futile, that life and death are mysteries that humankind has not fathomed, that no amount of reading will provide me with answers. The knowledge that I am seeking will have to emerge from within; it will have to be a felt knowledge, an experienced knowledge, not gleaned by way of the intellect.

If there is a God, then I have to experience that God directly, not rely on other people's writings, experiences or interpretations. I continue to read but now it is just a way of not being present to the moment, of not having to deal with the reality of what happened, of putting off the inevitable: acceptance of Ciara's death.

My mind is continually focused on Ciara and my desire to know where she is. Her image has been with me from the first moment of her disappearance. It is like a screensaver on a computer, constantly fixed in my head. I neither seek to retain it nor to let it go. It is beyond my control. It is just always there. It is there first thing when I wake up in the morning and last thing when I go to sleep. When I'm doing something that requires my concentrated focus my mind's eye becomes a split screen: I am focused on the task in the foreground and Ciara's image is always slightly behind and to the right. When I finish my task her image expands again to fill the screen.

This is not unwelcome in itself except that to be constantly fixed on her image also focuses me on her death. It is like an uncontrollable DVD playing over and over in my head and imprisoning me in a constant state of near panic.

A close friend tells me, by way of consolation, that it takes two years to get over the death of a loved one.

I shudder. Will it be possible to survive two years of this?

Solitude, silence and nature are now my preferred companions. I can no longer tolerate the abrasive world of humanity.

Today I sit in a park close to my home. I have hardly even noticed this park before, much less taken time to sit here. Life was always too busy, too full of activity. But now grief dictates the pace of my life. The minutes stretch into hours and the hours into days and somehow it must be got through. It must be endured. I am weighed down by my heavy blanket of sadness.

I feel the warmth of the sun on my skin. It does nothing to alleviate the tension I am holding in my body.

The bottlebrushes are in full bloom with their pendulous vials of nectar. The birds rustle in the leaves as they flit from branch to branch drinking nature's gift. The raspy two-tone call of the wattlebird penetrates my silence. 'She's gone,' it affirms. 'She's gone'. The cruel message echoes from tree to tree throughout the park, confirming what I already know but cannot grasp. The beauty and tranquillity of the world make a mockery of life. They trick us into believing that life is benevolent. Just when we finally learn to relax in that belief, it is cruelly snatched away.

I gaze at the trees with their gnarled twisted roots and their sturdy trunks towering above me into the blue sky. How old are they, older than Ciara was, older than I am now? How many eyes have looked upon those trees that now no longer see? How puny we are! How insignificant! And yet we strut the stage of life as if we are important, as if we are the centre of it all.

On my way home I stop outside a large old house. As I stare at the silent walls I imagine the sound of children's laughter echoing through the building. How many generations have passed through those doors and where are they now? They are no more and yet the house remains.

What are we when even the structures we build outlast us?

THE ANAESTHESIA OF SHOCK HAS worn off now. Searching for answers through reading proved futile. I have no choice but to face the raw reality of what happened and what is now. The enormity of it is just too much for my psyche to cope with. I have to sit with it and allow it to be absorbed gradually.

Every so often I take a break from the distraction of reading and allow myself to think of Ciara, that bright happy girl so full of life and who now no longer exists on this earth. Each time I allow myself to think of her the ache of the loss goes deeper. How much deeper can it go? Yet, I know I cannot avoid it or deny it, I must let it seep to the very core of my being before I can perhaps begin to accept it.

Life doesn't make sense anymore. I have read widely, sought out and talked with 'experts' and 'gurus' from the various religions – mainstream, periphery and alternative, yet nothing or no one can penetrate my prison of darkness and offer even a ray of hope.

I cannot see a way out of my despair. I have nowhere left to turn. I have been brought to my knees.

In desperation I begin to pray. 'Give me a sign Lord that Ciara is all right, I will be all right, I just need to know that Ciara is all right.' My prayer becomes a mantra that is repeated over and over again in my mind. Every waking moment, if my mind is not otherwise occupied, I automatically revert to my mantra.

My ability to continue living depends on an answer to my prayer. 'Jesus, you said Ask and you shall receive. Well, I'm asking you, I'm begging you, please give me a sign.'

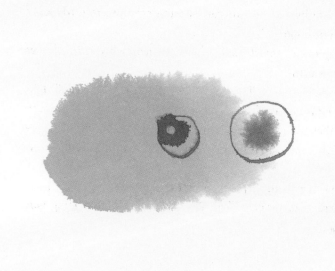

I NOW BEGIN EACH DAY by attending Mass in the private chapel of the nearby Presentation convent. I have taught with the Presentation nuns for almost twenty years. Most of those I taught with have either retired or transferred to other roles in the community. These caring women have opened their hearts and the door of their home to our family and given me a reason to rise and dress each morning. Spending time in solitude but not alone in the convent chapel imbues me with a sense of calm.

After Mass they always make time to talk for however long I choose. They do not waste words but speak with wisdom and insight. They have a very reassuring view about life and death. They radiate love and kindness and an inner peace. Just being in their presence provides me with respite from the inner turmoil that continually consumes me. I understand the importance of these caring women to my life.

But away from the atmosphere of the convent, the chaos returns with just as much force as before. Soon I will have to return to work and it will no longer be possible to start the day in this peaceful, comforting way.

People seldom see the halting and painful steps by which the most insignificant success is achieved.

ANNE SULLIVAN

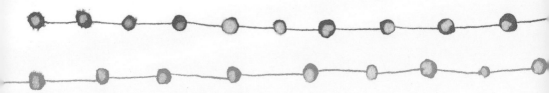

I RETURN TO TEACHING IN a Catholic girls secondary school. I am acutely conscious of the fact that I must not take my burden of grief into the classroom. My students deserve my full attention and I am determined they will get it. They must never for a moment be aware of the truth: that I have no interest in life, that my heart has atrophied, that I am dead inside.

Before entering a classroom I stop and steel myself for the task ahead. I breathe deeply and turn on a smile.

Despite my good intentions my resolve is often tested to its limit. This is the school Ciara attended and memories of her lie in wait around every corner.

I have a new student in one of my senior classes. I am taken aback to find her name is Ciara. In almost thirty years of teaching I have never encountered another Ciara. The sight of her sitting in front of me in her school uniform, as my daughter had done some ten years earlier, sends a dagger through my heart and throws me off balance.

It requires great effort to even say her name.

THIS YEAR I HAVE BEEN given a Religious Education class to teach. It was simply included in my timetable. I have never taught this subject before.

Lesson preparation for and teaching this subject bring me into daily conflict with my beliefs in the light of what has happened in my life. I am still silently crying out to God for a sign that Ciara is all right but at the same time questioning the very existence of this God who let me down so completely, in such a devastating way. If God is omnipotent, why didn't He keep Ciara safe? If He is all-loving, how can He stand by and watch humanity suffer so much?

I pick up the New Testament to begin some background reading for a lesson preparation. As I open the book at a familiar passage, the words suddenly appear to come towards me like the zoom through a telephoto lens. They appear larger and clearer and brighter. It is as if I am reading them for the first time, at a different level of understanding. I continue to read, unable to put down the book.

Jesus showed us in no uncertain way by His crucifixion and death that this is a suffering world: that we will all suffer, that suffering is somehow embedded in the very blueprint of humanity. The nature of this life could not have been demonstrated more clearly. The crucifixion, the cross, the symbol of Christianity, is the door through which we must all pass.

The absurdity of the crucifixion does have meaning after all.

SOMETIME LATER I AM TEACHING my first-year Religious Education class. We are studying the Ten Commandments. Today we come to the Fifth Commandment, Thou shalt not kill. We discuss the Commandment and all its implication in our daily lives. Eventually we come to its ultimate meaning—the killing of a fellow human being. One of the students asks, 'What if somebody kills somebody, does God forgive him?' I am brought to the quick. I pause before answering, 'Yes, God forgives everything if we are truly sorry.' Then another student adds, 'But what if somebody is really bad and kills two people, will God forgive him?' I answer again, 'Yes, if we are genuinely sorry for what we have done, God forgives.'

But I am to be tested a third time, when another student asks, 'But what if the person is really, really bad and kills three people, will God forgive him?'

I am forced to take a deep breath and pause before answering. Ciara's killer is thought to have killed two other young women before her. I answer again, 'Nothing is unforgivable in the eyes of God providing we are truly repentant for what we've done.'

There is no escape from this terrible tragedy. It shadows every aspect of my life.

Nevertheless it is good for me to be here among the young, who are immersed in life and possibility. They are attentive in class and they visit me privately to seek my advice or simply to have a sympathetic ear. It is as if they sense my receptivity and vulnerability as many of them share their private hurts and confide experiences they have never disclosed to anyone else. My life begins to have purpose again. Even if I can never enjoy life again I can still be of service to others.

I am grateful for the life-giving energy of these young people. Through them I am forced to reconnect with life, if only for a short time each day.

BACK AT WORK NOW, I realise that my eyesight has deteriorated significantly since Ciara's death. I am forced to wear glasses all the time but this does not solve my problem. My vision is still blurred and indistinct. I am constantly cleaning my lenses and clearing my eyes.

I return several times to the optometrist only to be assured that the prescription is correct and there is nothing wrong with my glasses.

It takes a long time for me to realise that my problem has nothing to do with deteriorating sight or my new glasses. It is my misty eyes permanently filled with uncryable tears.

Grief affects us in ways that we would never anticipate.

OUR TRAGEDY IS SO PUBLIC that there is no escape in Perth. We are recognised everywhere we go. The moment people see us, hear or see our name, they visibly flinch. Most offer their sympathy and for many the recognition appears to give them the freedom to tell their own grief stories and makes the expression of sorrow a more normal and natural thing. Many times in banks, shops and other public places, total strangers just pour out their sorrows. Even friends and work associates feel a new freedom to relate their stories of sadness.

This enables me to see that we are not alone. That many, many people are carrying similar, some heavier, burdens.

It further confirms my belief that we live in a suffering world. Somehow, for inexplicable reasons, suffering is an integral part of the human condition. We cannot escape it.

Not I, nor anyone else
can travel that road for you.
You must travel it yourself.

WALT WHITMAN

My husband carries his own burden. As a businessman he travels frequently overseas and interstate. When he comes home he returns to a wife who is not present.

The police are constantly in touch with him. The media seeks his opinion on every apparent development or rumour in the investigation. He appears strong, calm and measured but the deep lines etched on his face and the sad eyes tell a different story. He is hurting deeply. On the weekends he frequently disappears to our yacht for hours at a time. I know he goes there to weep, undisturbed and in private.

We each grieve in our own way, separately, differently and alone. We do not interfere with, criticise or judge each other. We are travelling side by side on parallel journeys and our paths do not meet. This is a lonely, private, isolating journey and we must travel it alone.

Our house now feels like a mausoleum. Death stares at us from every room.

Our study is next to Ciara's bedroom. Denis never enters it now. He never ventures downstairs to that part of the house any more. He would like to sell and move house, to get away from the constant reminders. I am reluctant. Will the house bring us comforting memories of Ciara sometime in the future? I cannot take the chance of depriving us of that possibility and so we decide to stay in the house, with all its painful memories.

What is life?
It is the flash of a firefly in the night.
It is the breath of a buffalo in the winter time.
It is the little shadow which runs across the grass
And loses itself in the sunset.

CRAWFOOT (BLACKFOOT)

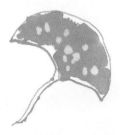

IT IS SATURDAY MORNING. As the dawn light steals across the sky, pushing before it the last vastitudes of darkness, the birds begin to welcome a new day. I do not share their enthusiasm. Sadness leaves my body heavy and lethargic. My mind is focused on the moment. The past is too painful, the future too uncertain. The present moment is all I can deal with now. I lie, listless and empty, reluctant to get out of bed.

Suddenly I am aware that I am floating upwards. My body remains on the bed but I am rising higher and higher towards the ceiling. As I am just about to touch the ceiling I am gripped by fear and I return instantly to my body.

I spend some time reflecting on what has just occurred.

Clearly I am not my body. My body is merely the shell that encases the essence of who and what I really am. When I was floating to the ceiling I was whole and entire, with my mind, my thoughts, my awareness and even my fears. What remained on the bed was merely a shell, nothing more than a piece of discarded clothing.

Is this then what death is? A discarding of the visible component of who and what I am, the part that holds me earthbound? Does Ciara then, still exist whole and entire somewhere beyond my sight?

I believe so. Now I know that death is not the end. It is not to be feared. It is nothing more than the discarding of the human form, so that we can return to where we came from.

I believe that I have been given this experience to help me understand that death is merely a transition from this existence to the next. This experience brings me a step closer to being at peace with Ciara's death.

We are, in the words of Teilhard de Chardin, *spiritual beings having a human experience.*

Where there is great love
there are always miracles.

WILLA CATHER

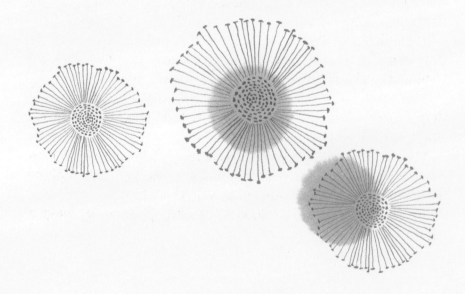

It is Saturday again, another day without the respite of work. I lie in bed, wide awake, knowing I will soon have to get up and face yet another day of desolation. Today is going to be particularly difficult. Some very good friends have asked us to take them to the place where Ciara's body was found. They want to pay their respects there.

I lie with my eyes closed, without thought. Thoughts are too painful. Suddenly words appear before my closed eyes, letters written in white on the dark background of my sightlessness. They move across like breaking news on a TV screen. 'It's nothing, don't cry,' they say. They circle again and again and I recognise Ciara's handwriting. Is it possible that this is a message from Ciara? I am sceptical.

Puzzled, I get out of bed and go downstairs to the filing cabinet and find her last letter. The writing in the mysterious message is still clearly etched in my mind. Sure enough, that is how she makes a 'y' and that is her 'r'. The writing is unmistakably Ciara's—the words are from her. My spirits are lifted and I face the day with new vigour.

A couple of days later the phenomenon is repeated, only this time the words appear out of a swirl of mauve. The letters are in black and in typescript clearly visible on the mauve background. The word 'peace' appears and the word 'live', then later, the words 'love' and 'joy'.

I do not understand what's happening but I am strangely consoled and uplifted by it. I try not to dwell on it as I am sceptical of anything I do not understand.

In the ensuing days and weeks I mention my experience to various people. The reactions I receive are a mix of pity, puzzlement and incredulity. Could it be that people think I am so grief-stricken that I am hallucinating or are they, like me, simply wary of anything they cannot rationalise? I decide to be more discerning about who I tell in the future. The phenomenon continues.

IT IS NOW FIVE MONTHS since Ciara's death. The pain does not ease. I try to reconnect with the flow of life but I cannot. It is impossible to enjoy anything.

Tonight we sleep on our yacht. I wake up in the middle of the night, consumed by grief as always. Suddenly I detect a beautiful fragrance. Where is it coming from? We are on a yacht surrounded by water and there are no flowers or perfume on board.

I do not connect the fragrance with Ciara but it takes my mind off my all-consuming sadness and I drift back to sleep under the spell of its delicate bouquet.

In the morning I wonder fleetingly where the perfume came from. But I don't dwell on it and believe that I will find out in time.

Love never fails.

1 Corinthians 13:8

CIARA'S BEDROOM REMAINS UNCHANGED, untouched, gathering dust. It was once a room that even in her absence was animated by her vibrancy. I am drawn to the door in the hope of recapturing that vital energy, but once I open it I see only a hollow, lifeless room full of reminders that she is no longer with us, no longer a life force. It is a room to be generally avoided, to be entered only when one feels strong enough to do so.

Today is one such day. Denis is overseas on business. Denise is coming to help pack up Ciara's belongings. I have braced myself for what is in store. The packing cases are ready. We set aside one 'memory box' for her most loved items. We systematically go through her clothes and with one last lingering look at each item we reverently fold it and pack it away for the last time. Each item carries its own special memory: the orange and black beach wrap with the Egyptian motif, the hot pink ski pants, her first business suit. It is a very painful process but we persevere in the knowledge that it has to be done and not by a stranger. We do not allow ourselves the indulgence of reminiscing, for we know that if we did we would never finish. It would become unbearable.

We finally finish, close the boxes and leave them in the bedroom. One of the charitable organisations will come tomorrow to collect them.

Denise returns to her home.

I am alone. I feel utterly drained, emotionally depleted.

Later in the evening I am drawn again to Ciara's room. As I stand looking at her life packed up in a few boxes, I become conscious of a beautiful fragrance. It is faint at first but slowly increases in intensity. It is an intoxicating perfume and appears to ebb and flow. I move away from the packing cases; the perfume is not there. I move back again; the perfume is there. It is only in the vicinity of her belongings. I am totally perplexed by this phenomenon. Where has it come from? It is strangely consoling.

I spend some time breathing in deeply this perfume-filled air and bask in its unction. Soon the perfume dissipates but its comforting effect lingers.

My experiences continue. Every couple of days I am gifted with a new 'vision'. I see the words 'love' and 'joy'. Then one day I see a pinprick of light in the darkness of my closed eyes and as the pinprick expands it forms a heart shape and inside the heart shape Ciara's head and shoulders appear. She is smiling and turns her head from side to side.

On another occasion I see her standing beside a huge silver trophy. She is dressed in red—a colour she never wore.

These experiences buoy me for a time but then I lapse back into my state of despair with the added burden of the uncertainty they present. Could I be hallucinating? Is there any explanation? My family is very accepting of what is happening but they cannot explain it either.

Eventually I tell a friend, whose reaction is one of acceptance. 'Yes,' she says, 'I believe this can happen because when my mother died I got a beautiful smell of roses from her casket'.

I recall my perfume experiences and I begin to fit the pieces together. My mood changes from scepticism to possibility. Something out of the ordinary is obviously happening, something beyond me, something beyond normal possibility, and yet I dare not allow myself to believe this.

I return to my reading. To my surprise and relief I find numerous accounts of experiences such as mine. Recordings of such events have been well documented. How could I not have known this before?

I am elated. I know now with certainty that there is no death and that Ciara still exists. I know that there is a God and that He has answered my prayers. I want to shout it aloud, to let everybody know.

But not everyone shares my elation or conviction. I am still met with the same looks of disbelief, some bordering on pity. Just as my previous reading failed to provide consolation for me, so too does another's experience fail to convince.

I now realise that only the experience itself has the power to convince.

*The most beautiful experience we can have
is the mysterious.*

ALBERT EINSTEIN

I ARRIVE HOME AFTER A weary day at work. I open the door of the living area and am greeted by a wave of perfume. It is so intense that it halts me in my tracks. I search for its source. There is a vase of roses on the table. I remove it to the dining room and close the door firmly. The beautiful perfume remains. I am compelled to comprehend this.

I am much more open and receptive now. Gone is the fear, the inclination towards disbelief, towards resistance.

I move around the house and the perfume accompanies me. It is real. It is almost tangible. Someone or something is trying to communicate something beautiful to me. Finally, I sit and allow myself to receive.

I sense an electrifying of the air, a silent buzzing, a palpable presence. I inhale deeply and I experience a profound peace, an inner joy. I find myself smiling for the first time since Ciara's death. The remainder of the evening is passed in an aura of peaceful bliss.

I attend a formal dinner where my husband is one of the guests of honour. He is overseas and I am representing him. I am reluctant to leave the beautiful perfume but to my surprise it accompanies me and sustains my buoyant spirits throughout the evening.

I wake up the following morning to its healing presence. It accompanies me to work and remains with me all day. For three days it is my constant companion. By this time all doubts have evaporated.

*What a gift of grace to be able to
take the chaos from within and from it
create some semblance of order.*

KATHERINE PATERSON

THE EXPERIENCE IS TOO REAL for me to deny any more. I no longer need confirmation from books. The views of others have become less important or meaningful. I alone know the truth of what is happening. I hold the experience deep inside *like a pearl of great price*, only to be taken out and polished when I am alone or shared with my family and trusted friends. I feel singularly blessed.

I know that wherever Ciara is or whatever she is experiencing has to be beautiful, because only something beautiful could emit such an intoxicating fragrance and generate such inner peace and joy.

God has answered my prayers. I have a feeling of being held and cared for and that God is in control.

I am at peace with the question of Ciara's whereabouts now but I am not at peace with her absence.

Over me soared the eternal sky,
Full of light and deity;
Again I saw, again I heard,
The rolling river, the morning bird;–
Beauty through my senses stole;
I yielded myself to the perfect whole.

RALPH WALDO EMERSON

THE LIGHT OF MY WORLD has been turned on again, brighter and more intense than ever. I have a heightened awareness of and sensitivity to the colours, beauty and sounds of nature. Everything joins me in mourning the passing of Ciara. Flowers and trees reach out to tell me of their sorrow, birds venture close and convey their messages of hope, the soft rain drenches the air with its tears, even the gentle breeze as it caresses my skin tells me of its sadness. Nature envelops me in its soothing balm. It exudes gentleness, care, support, empathy.

I am deeply aware of the interconnectedness and sacredness of all things. I am but a part of it all, no more, no less, and we are all part of a greater whole.

I am experiencing life vitality through the darkness of my grief.

When the heart weeps for what it has lost
the soul laughs for what it has found.

Sufi Aphorism

I NOW LIVE A PARADOX. Concepts I once considered mutually exclusive—life and death, joy and sorrow, consolation and desolation—have now merged and I experience both simultaneously. It is not a fluctuation between the two but a strange co-existence of both. On the surface I am sad and despondent, still utterly devastated by the loss of Ciara, but underneath I am excited, even joyous, buoyed by a sense of presence, by the realisation that I am not alone, that I am being held and cared for, that someone or something far greater than me is in control and I need not fear. I do not fear death any more. I am convinced that death is not annihilation, only a transition from this part of our existence to the next.

I know that Ciara still exists in a state or realm not accessible to us, that she is already where we will all be one day.

I am conscious of the eternal nature of all things and the brevity of our time here on earth. I am aware that we will never again have that earthbound mother-daughter relationship. But we will be united again in a bond of love that lies beyond our limited understanding.

My task now is to be available for the other members of my family and to do whatever good I can for whatever time is left to me on this earth.

How DO I EXPLAIN THIS strange co-existence of opposites that is taking place within me? Is there two of me or has part of me somehow been able to tap into the divine that is the essence of us all, the other part remaining firmly connected to the physical world? I do not know.

All I know is that deep down I am singing for joy while another part of me is still in the depths of sadness. This sadness encompasses much more than my own feelings of loss. It encompasses also my grief for the way Ciara's life ended, for the terrible trauma she would have suffered, for the future that was snatched from her, for the opportunities to love and be loved that were denied her, for the husband and children she will never have, for the lost opportunities to gain wisdom and insight as she journeyed through life.

It includes my grief for her sister, for the void that is left in her life, for my future grandchildren, who will never know their mother's only sibling.

I grieve also for the fact that I am powerless to assuage my husband's sadness.

All this is as much a part of my grief as my own loneliness and hurt.

EVERY DAY IS AN ANNIVERSARY.

Thursday—the last evening we spent together and the day her body was found.

Friday—the last time I saw her and the day of her funeral.

Saturday—the day of realisation that we would never see her again.

And so it continues.

Days that are meant to be days of celebration are now days tinged with sadness. There is always someone missing, a conspicuous absence, an empty chair, a silenced voice in the conversation.

We do not speak about her but our silence speaks louder than words. We miss her acutely. Nothing can fill the void of her absence. It is a constant companion.

Gone—flitted away,
Taken the stars from the night,
And the sun from the day!
Gone—and a cloud in my heart.

ALFRED LORD TENNYSON

THE IMAGE OF CIARA IS beginning to fade. It is distant, blurred, out of focus now. I strain to bring it forward, to sharpen the focus. But it remains at a fixed distance, moving backwards at exactly the same rate as I move forward.

Occasionally I manage to conjure up a vivid image of her, only to be disappointed by the realisation that it is an image of a photograph I have of her.

I try to recall her voice, her laughter, but they elude me.

The living, breathing Ciara is fading from my memory. The past, no matter how precious, cannot be held.

Surely, this is the second death.

I AM FILLED WITH AN insatiable longing, an aching for Ciara. I want to see her again, to hear her laughter, to inhale her fragrance. I want to know where she is and what she is doing. I want to reach out and touch her, to feel her body, but there is no one there; only an empty space, a gaping hole.

I know now how an amputee must feel when a limb is severed and the brain doesn't register its removal. It continues to send signals to the missing limb but there is nothing there to respond. I have had an emotional amputation. That part of me that was nourished by the bond of love between Ciara and me is no longer nourished and I am left with an unrequited emotional craving. No other member of my family can satisfy that longing.

The unfilled longing builds up to a crescendo and forces me to retreat to a quiet space where I can contemplate her, where I can go back in time to a place where all was well, where our family was intact, where Ciara was with us.

The outcome of this time travel is twofold. While it releases the valve of longing it also increases the awareness of what is now missing. My intense longing is only replaced by a deeper sorrow.

MOTHERHOOD COMES AT A PRICE. Becoming a mother is a joyous experience yet also a burdensome responsibility. We wear motherhood like a jewel but also like a dagger for the remainder of our lives. We are never separated from it. We rejoice with each joy experienced by our children. We suffer with every hurt but our suffering is intensified by our lack of control.

Our children grow up; they leave home, get married and have children of their own. Intellectually we know they are independent. They must be allowed to be free. Outwardly we acknowledge and accommodate this but how do we tell our hearts? What language do we use to convince the heart? It is still connected. It still clings, still aches and still rejoices. Even over the chasm of death it still longs.

I know now that when Ciara was born only a physical separation took place. I remain bonded emotionally to her. That bond can never be severed. It is part of my very being. The love that flowed between us is as important to my emotional wellbeing as the blood that flows through my veins is to my physical health.

Is it possible that there is some as yet unidentified connection between mother and child? This then would account for the endless aching, the endless longing.

IT IS NOW THREE YEARS since Ciara's death. The groundswell of people who rallied round after her death has long gone. They have returned to their busy lives. I feel completely alone. My life has collapsed again into an abyss of nothingness, a monotony of meaninglessness. The only emotion I feel is profound sadness. I have no interest in anything. This includes my appearance. I wear the minimum amount of makeup; eye makeup only irritates my permanently teary eyes. Jewellery holds no interest for me. I have not changed my earrings for three years. I wear a simple gold chain and a gold cross around my neck. The chain belonged to Ciara and the cross reminds me of the suffering Jesus. I do not wear perfume. I don't want any earthly smells interfering with my still occasional mysterious visits. I haven't bought any clothes in three years. I make do with what I have but I am putting on weight.

The effort of keeping up appearances during my working day saps all my energy and I retreat to my home in the evenings with my head reeling from the seemingly endless chatter of the day. My evenings are spent reading. I do not watch TV. The news programmes frequently contain some report about the investigation into Ciara's murder and most of the other programmes contain some aspect of violence. I can't bear to watch violence.

I still keep the doors and windows of the house firmly locked.

Ciara occasionally speaks to me out of death's wide silence with her perfumed message of peace, but God is very distant. Gone is the feeling of presence, of being carried and held. I make every effort to reinstate it. I meditate; I attend Church; I pray, but all to no avail. All that remains is the sweet memory of it. It is just enough to get me out of bed each morning and to put one foot in front of the other.

I feel totally abandoned. My heartfelt prayers of anguish meet a brick wall of silence and are returned to me with increased helplessness. I do not doubt the existence of God. My past experiences have been too real, too vivid, to allow me to do that. It is more that God has withdrawn from me and I feel empty.

What do I mean by 'God'? What is the purpose of life? These questions occupy my mind and my time as I search desperately for answers. If life has no purpose then why am I here?

Denis tries to keep the spark of life alive in me. He is my anchor. He arranges to meet friends, he books holidays and weekends away. He realises the importance of remaining engaged with life. I go along because I do not have the capacity to do otherwise but nothing has the power to jolt me out of my misery.

As I SEARCH FRUITLESSLY FOR answers to my questions, the name Ain Karim keeps cropping up in conversations with people from diverse walks of life. I have heard the name so often now that I follow my inner promptings and make further inquiries. I discover that it is a retreat centre in Bridgetown, south of Perth. I book in for a week-long silent retreat. The retreat is due to begin on Easter Monday but I decide to go on the Thursday before and spend Easter there. Easter is a particularly difficult time because this is when Ciara was missing. In all I will have eleven days of solitude and silence at the retreat centre—a welcome respite.

From the moment I arrive I am enveloped in an atmosphere of kindness, support and caring. Silence, prayer and reflection are the main focus of the retreat, with a daily visit from the retreat director. I pass my days reflecting, weeping, reading spiritual material, but mostly I pray. 'Free me from this hurt Lord,' I silently cry with utter abandonment, because I have no other choice. I am just one step away from utter despair.

By the Wednesday I hit rock bottom. I am convinced that there is nothing here for me, that all of this is just mumbo jumbo. I can't take any more of it. I just want to pack my bag and return home immediately. If I leave now I will be home by late afternoon. But how can I explain my sudden departure to the retreat director? She allowed me to come four days early, I now realise, at great personal inconvenience. She fitted me in at short notice when she already had a full house, and since my arrival her kindness to me has shown no limits. I cannot be so ungracious and just leave for no other reason than my own selfishness. I decide to stay and complete the week as planned, even though I no longer want to be here.

Later in the day I am standing in my room feeling completely dejected, not knowing where to turn or what to do. Suddenly a transformation begins to take place, the tight vice grip of grief begins to loosen, the heavy weight lifts from my shoulders, my face begins to relax and my eyes open wider, my clenched fingers relax and I feel unburdened. The transformation unfolds as if in slow motion and is similar to what I had experienced that morning during Mass following Ciara's disappearance, when all my physical pain was removed. The contrast is significant. I hadn't realised how constricted I had been for the past three years by my heavy straightjacket of grief. I had forgotten what it was like to feel free. Once again I am convinced that what has just occurred is something beyond my control. God has tangibly returned to my life and my mood changes. I am elated and so grateful for what has occurred. Once again my prayers have been answered, and in a very convincing way.

But soon doubt begins to find its way back into my thinking. Is this just a temporary reprieve? Will it all come back again when I return to Perth, to all the reminders, to the police investigation and the unrelenting media interest?

If you want to know the truth
I will tell you the truth.
Friend, listen: the God whom
I love is inside.

Kabir

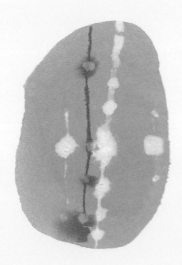

I HAVE NEVER BEFORE EXPERIENCED God in such a personal, tangible way and I am at a loss to understand it.

I spend the remainder of my time at the retreat centre in silent contemplation of the mystery of life and the mystery of God.

Suddenly, in the middle of the night, I am jolted out of my sleep with the words "there is only God", and I understand with absolute clarity that this is indeed so. The universe does not exist outside of God. Everything is in God and God is in everything and God is in me. Why didn't I grasp this before?

Thomas Aquinas's words *God is existence* are absolutely true.

Once again I realise that this mystery is so profound, so deep, that the certainty of it has to come from a deeper consciousness. It has to come from within.

The image of the unseen God
in whom were created
all things in heaven and on earth:
everything visible and everything invisible,
in Him all things hold together,
and through Him all things are reconciled.

COLOSSIANS 1: 15-17, 20

I FEEL LIBERATED. GOD IS no longer absent or remote but is to be found wherever I turn. God is unspeakably near yet vastly expansive and the whole universe is sacred. Every aspect of creation is a cell in the body of God and just as the cells in my own body are interconnected and interdependent so too is all of the universe. It is one enormous web of life and it is all God. Creating, renewing, healing and restoring. Our role is to live out of that knowledge and to simply cooperate. We can help maintain the balance and harmony of this great universe by our thoughts and actions.

Human life does have meaning after all, however obscure that meaning is to our limited understanding. The mystery is no longer an obstacle to be probed and understood but an invitation to go deeper. I know I will never understand it completely while I am in human form but that does not mean I cannot experience a deeper meaning and a deeper relationship with God. I know this now with total conviction. I can breathe easily again.

I am still comfortable using the name God. For me now, the name evokes a relationship rather than an identity. It connotes peace, contentment, security, intimacy and encompassment, a feeling of being enveloped in love but also a feeling of wonder, awe and reverence.

I have a quiet confidence that a far greater picture is involved here. All I can do is surrender to the mystery and accept that ultimately, in the words of the great mystic Julian of Norwich, *all shall be well, all manner of things shall be well.*

I can learn to live again after all.

Even as the snow fell,
through it there came whispering,
a breath of Spring

KOBAYASHI ISSA

I RETURN TO PERTH. To my relief the overwhelming burden of sadness does not return.

Shortly after this my first grandchild is born. This is another turning point. Now, the image of Ciara, which although fading, has remained in my mind's eye, is replaced occasionally with the image of my new grandchild and I find a new interest in life.

I now experience short periods of respite where I can savour life again.

As the year passes the tension builds up once more. With the approach of Ciara's anniversary the media attention increases and I am forced to escape to the retreat centre again.

I am so grateful to have this quiet haven of support and understanding.

As I sit on the balcony outside my room at the retreat centre I can hear the voices of children playing at the nearby school. My thoughts drift to the person who murdered Ciara and the two other young women who were taken from the same area. Very shortly after Ciara's death I decided that this person had destroyed the life of one member of my family and I was not going to allow him to destroy another, so I had not allowed him to even enter my thoughts again until this moment.

The children's jollity arouses in me thoughts that I feel I could and should ponder. Was Ciara's murderer once a young child similar to these, full of laughter and fun? What terrible thing occurred in his life that caused his heart to close so that he could feel no love, no compassion for others? Or was he just born evil? Is he now living a carefree life, enjoying the world with all it has to offer, with no remorse or understanding of the enormity of his terrible deed? Certainly he is free of the restraints prison life would impose but is he really free, unconcerned about the beautiful lives he cut short, unaffected by the havoc he has caused to so many other people?

I decide that is impossible. No matter how much one tries to deny or suppress one's conscience, it is not possible to do so. It is an integral component of every person that in the end will always prevail. Ciara's murderer might not be in a physical prison but he is not free. Freedom has nothing to do with locks, bolts or walls. If the heart is not free one can never be free. What a terrible burden to carry. Moment by moment, hour by hour, day by day, he must be in continual torment. The guilt must remain in his consciousness like a malignant tumour, corroding his very soul. His heinous secret can never be revealed or shared. He must be forever vigilant lest any detail of his crime is unintentionally revealed. His punishment is a lifetime of guilt and secrecy. To live in the prison of our own conscience is surely the greatest of all torments.

I wonder if it is better to be free in our heart in the confines of a physical prison than to be free in the world but imprisoned in our heart. This contemplation leads me to the question of forgiveness. I can never exonerate or condone the actions of Ciara's murderer. What he did was wrong. Nothing can ever change that. But if forgiveness means letting him go to get on with his own life, then I have forgiven him already. Ultimately the question of forgiveness rests within himself. I am not the arbiter between him and his conscience. I cannot save him from the consequences of his actions. I decide never to spend time thinking of this person again.

The remainder of my time at the centre is spent continuing my journey of probing the deeper mysteries of life.

Who would have thought my shrivel'd heart
Could have recover'd greennesse? It was gone
Quite under ground.

GEORGE HERBERT

I CONTINUE TO RETURN TO this sanctuary annually until, regrettably, it closes down two years later.

This time of solitude is sacred time—a time for intense reflection.

Each time I return home again more healed, more alive, more connected with life, with humanity and with God. Gradually my respite periods become longer until eventually the balance shifts and I begin to feel more alive than dead.

Then one day six years after Ciara's death I smile again, a genuine heartfelt smile, and I know that life is beginning to return.

STRUGGLING THROUGH GRIEF IS LIKE struggling to swim to shore in a stormy sea. We are battered and bruised as we are thrown around in the powerful surge. We struggle to stay afloat as wave after wave swamps us relentlessly and drags us down, leaving us disoriented and wallowing in darkness in the turbulent waters. Our energy is sapped and at times we feel we will not survive. Our attention is focused on the raging waves and our struggle for air and we do not notice anything else that is going on around us. Even hands reaching out to help us go unnoticed as we thrash and struggle to remain afloat. Eventually exhaustion overcomes us and we are forced to submit to the relentless tide, for to continue to struggle against it is certain death. Our energy begins to return as we learn to give in to the pull of the waves.

At times we are submerged, at other times we are picked up and carried further towards the shore. We are not in control any more. All we can do is be receptive to what is happening and trust that the waves will eventually bring us to land.

We now begin to notice the hands reaching out to help and can muster sufficient energy and trust to grab on to some. Gradually the waves begin to subside. Now, when we bob to the surface, we catch glimpses of the shoreline in the distance.

Perhaps survival is possible after all.

SIBLINGS ARE OFTEN THE SILENT neglected following the death of a child. Everyone rallies around the parents. They, in turn, are so overwhelmed by their own grief that they are simply not fully present for their other children, particularly adult offspring who are often left to deal with their grief alone. Their young adult friends don't always know how to respond. Their hearts have not yet been opened to compassion as most of them have never been wounded. The dominant response is to avoid the issue altogether.

Denise is Ciara's only sibling; just fifteen months separated them and they were always 'best friends'. They were always together. Even when they studied very different courses at the same university they remained best friends. Ciara's friends were Denise's friends and Denise's friends were Ciara's. At the time of Ciara's death, Denise was employed as a registrar in a busy tertiary hospital. For a week she went to work each day knowing that her sister's body was lying in the same hospital. She had to endure the horrendous rumours about Ciara's death that were circulating throughout the hospital, not knowing if they were true.

In the first year after Ciara's death Denise was often called out in the middle of the night to attend to emergencies. How did she feel walking unescorted in the dark through the hospital car park knowing what had happened to her sister? During that time she was at the receiving end of threats from violent patients in the Emergency department. Yet she never faltered. She continued to go to work each day and to study for her physician's examination. When she requested her annual leave the year following Ciara's death, she was informed she had none left. In the confusion and chaos at the time of Ciara's death, she had neglected to fill in the necessary form to request compassionate leave and so her time off then was deemed to be holidays. Yet she never flinched, just continued to work without complaint. She later passed her physician's exam despite the terrible burden of grief she was carrying.

During this terrible time we all came to know Denise's fiancé, Ian, in a completely different way. He displayed a wisdom, strength and courage way beyond his years. He remained steadfast and unwavering and brought an aura of calm to a traumatic situation. How brave they both were to embark on their married life carrying the burden of Ciara's murder. This was a time when they should have been carefree, joyous, a time that can never be repeated in their lives. How difficult it must have been for them. Yet, I can see how they have grown through this. They both show a depth of character, wisdom and compassion, a sensitivity rarely seen in people their age. Nothing seems to destabilise them. They can cope in any situation. They are always at the ready when any of their friends experience difficulties. They are extraordinarily loving and patient parents to their four children and are extremely competent, responsible and caring specialists in their respective fields.

The maxim *strength comes through adversity* appears in their case to be so true.

IT IS ONLY IN TIMES of tragedy that the true meaning of family is fully experienced. Acquaintances and some friends will come and go as the seasons of life pass but the one constant that always can be depended upon is the family. Both Denis' and my family live overseas and while I was in contact by phone after Ciara death, I nevertheless felt their physical absence intensely.

Immediately after Ciara's death I had a pressing desire for my mother's presence, not especially for any words of wisdom or consolation she might impart but simply for her presence. Even though my mother had died three years earlier, that desire remained with me for some time. Is this another sign of that unidentified connection that might exist between mother and child?

My sister's and my two nieces' company during that terrible time when Ciara was missing was a great blessing. They tolerated, without question, my complete detachment and my inability to be present. Their generous, selfless and undemanding presence each day provided the support I so desperately needed at that time. Only family would make the time to be so completely and unselfishly available. My brother and nephew and two brothers-in-law travelled from Ireland to farewell Ciara and to be a supportive presence at the funeral. Even though my brother's other son was gravely ill in hospital in Ireland at the time, he still made the journey. We were not capable of welcoming or entertaining them as we would have done under different circumstances. Their generosity of spirit will always be remembered with gratitude. Back in Ireland both Denis' family and mine held prayer services for Ciara and opened their houses to the many people who came to express their condolences. The support from so many in Ireland was overwhelming and uplifting.

We greatly appreciated the many and very frequent phone calls from family members in the months and years following Ciara's death. In a sense Ciara's death has brought us even closer together.

Another great blessing that has occurred in our lives is the friendship of our daughter's parents-in-law. They are very kind and thoughtful people who have embraced us as part of their family, as indeed has their extended family. We share four beautiful grandchildren whose existence is a constant delight to us and which further strengthens the bond of friendship that has developed between us.

IT IS NOW ELEVEN YEARS since Ciara's death. Time has distanced me from the rawness of the pain but the wound continues to weep secretly and silently in the depths of my being. Every so often a profound sadness and longing well up from deep inside and spill over into uncontrollable silent convulsions of sobbing. This can be triggered by the most unexpected things: a piece of music, a beautiful scene, a girl who reminds me of Ciara or just the sight of young people enjoying life. Thankfully these episodes are short-lived and I have learned to avoid as far as possible the triggering events.

One thing I cannot avoid is the endless media interest in and coverage of Ciara's murder. Each time I feel I am coming out of the darkness, I suffer a major setback as a direct result of some 'new' media interest. The wound is then reopened in all its rawness and I am sent hurtling back into the abyss. Simply refusing to watch the television programme or read the news articles or book about the murder does not shield me because invariably the journalists first approach us seeking our comments or our participation. Then weeks and even months of anguish go by until the telecast or publication takes place. These in turn ignite a further spate of media interest and the whole event is replayed all over again. After a few weeks the frenzy ceases and we are left again to try to rebuild our lives, until the next time.

There are some exceptions to the insensitivity of the media. One of the many hundreds of letters we received and greatly appreciated was from a newsreader who took the time to write to us one evening before going to air with the news. It was a beautifully sensitive letter. A couple of other journalists keep in touch in a caring, helpful way. They demonstrate it is possible to be a successful journalist and to practise compassion.

What kind of world have we created when violence and murder become the subjects of entertainment?

OUR FOUR GRANDCHILDREN BRING ME immeasurable joy.

A mother's love is always tempered by the responsibility of caring for and nurturing her children, while a grandmother is free to love unencumbered. Sometimes I even surprise myself by the depth of emotion my grandchildren are capable of engendering in me. It is a mix of love, reverence, wonder and gratitude for their existence. My heart melts every time I see them as their smiles of welcome light up their faces. The joy of life dances in their eyes. I marvel at and learn from them. Their innocent, unimpaired exuberance for life, their total trust, honesty and openness, reassure me of the goodness of humanity. Just being in their presence is an exercise in contemplation. They give me their full attention and in turn they expect mine. Observing their unwavering concentration as they study a picture in a book or build a Lego model is a lesson in practising mindfulness. They are completely in the present moment.

Their questions force me to rethink my fixed ideas and opinions and make me realise how important it is to keep my thinking fluid, ready to move with the flow of life. They readily climb on my knee and snuggle in as we hold each other. 'I love you Grandma' slips easily from their lips. They have no inhibitions, no reservations; they have not yet begun to erect the barriers around them that we deem necessary to navigate the human world.

Their personalities and interests are so different yet they have been nurtured in the same household. It is as if some inner light is shining through, guiding them on their respective paths.

This is where I am nourished, where I gain my strength, where I continue to regain my equilibrium. This is where I want to be.

Day by day, bit by bit,
Pain drips from the heart
As against our will
And even in our own despite
Comes wisdom
From the awful grace of the gods.

AESCHYLUS

THIS BOOK HAS BEEN NINE years in the writing. I wondered why it was taking me so long to finish. Then I realised I was unwittingly waiting for some definitive end to come to my grieving. I was waiting to wake up one morning and be able to say, it's over, now I can resume my life.

Now I know it can never be over. There can never be any going back to the life we lived before Ciara's death. Life has changed now. It has lost its innocence. This is not like a movie where I can temporarily be shocked and repulsed by the horror and evil in the world, be moved to tears by the sadness, then the movie ends and I go home and get on with life. This is life and it is my life now. I have tasted the woundedness, the evil and the horror of the world in a way that has changed me forever.

Life is not meant to be static. We are meant to change and grow. Through my encounter with man's inhumanity to man I have experienced deep grief but also, and paradoxically, tremendous growth. But the movie never ends.

Truth is one,
The sages speak of it by many names.

Vedic Scripture

I WILL ALWAYS BE GRATEFUL for my Catholic upbringing. It kept me grounded when my entire world had fallen apart. It later provided a base from which to explore the mystery of life and death and it kept drawing me back when I wandered off on some obscure tangent. The spark of hope that sustained me during that long, dark winter of grief and doubt was ignited and sustained by the solid foundation of my faith. All my life I believed that life had a meaning above and beyond our physical existence. This belief was severely tested, battered and shaken but it was never completely extinguished. It guided me through the darkest of times.

All religions are the expression of that one basic search in the human heart—the search for meaning. Most religions have the same fundamental credence, that there is a universal power that animates all life. Religion is humanity's attempt at understanding and interpreting that fundamental credence. God is simply the name we give to that ineffable universal force, our attempt at naming the unnameable. We can deny God, refuse to acknowledge God's existence and even belittle those who do, but the fundamental reality remains that without God there is nothing. Albert Einstein's wisdom was profound in this regard when he said, *Called or not, God is always present.*

All religions reduce God to fit human intelligence and frequently to meet human expectations. They are all subject to human frailties. Religion can nevertheless provide a helpful roadmap for embarking on a spiritual journey. This journey often begins with knowledge acquired through a belief system but it should not end there. It needs to be converted by experience if we are to grow as spiritual beings. The surest way of attaining this is through suffering. Suffering is the key to unlocking our understanding.

GRIEF HAS TAUGHT ME THE value of living in the present moment. It robbed me of my past, for to contemplate the past is to cause pain. It denied me a future, as I am keenly aware that the future cannot be controlled or necessarily guaranteed. So I am forced to remain in the present, the only moment where I can truly experience life.

Living decisively in the moment dissolves my chattering mind, leaving a silent space into which flow a quiet peace, a joy and an awareness of the privilege that is life. My attention is expanded beyond myself. I see everything around me in a new light. Everything has become more intense, more vivid and more alive. Everything is felt at a depth I did not know existed before; sorrow, joy, wonder, awe, peace, love, gratitude, empathy, well-up and spill over in a way I had never thought possible.

Living out of this space, my fears have dissolved because what gives rise to fear is past experiences and uncertainty about what might happen in the future.

I notice that things happen effortlessly. When a problem arises I intuitively know what to do, I do it and then leave it behind. It is as if I am being guided.

Life has become peaceful and effortless. Nothing can destabilise me anymore.

Your pain is the breaking of the shell that enclo∫es your under∫tanding.

KAHLIL GIBRAN

TWELVE YEARS HAVE NOW PASSED since Ciara was taken from us and I have finally emerged into the sunlight. But I am a different person. A tremendous growth has taken place during my long winter of exile. Ciara's death gave me new eyes through which to evaluate my own life and I am grateful for all I have learned. If only I could have done so without Ciara's death.

I see life more clearly now. I see through and beyond the artificial and imposed barriers to life, barriers that envelop us like smog and prevent us from experiencing and enjoying life to the full. I live life simply, swimming in the ocean of beauty which surrounds me, drinking in the nectar of nature, melting into its harmony, the sweet sound of bird song, the gentle whisper of the wind as it rustles in the leaves, the lapping of the ocean.

I have accepted Ciara's death. We cannot change the course of life; we can only change ourselves. I know that Ciara has merely moved on to the next phase of her eternity, as all of us will.

I have become piercingly aware of the beauty that surrounds me, of the hidden dialogue that takes place between all things and the unseen thread that connects all. I have become sensitised to the suffering world, not just the suffering of humanity but the suffering of all living things, and I cannot cause pain to anything. Past suffering is still there but it is integrated into who I have become and no longer weighs me down. I know that for whatever reason, suffering and joy go hand in hand. If I am prepared to accept one, must I not also be prepared to accept the other? We can only experience through opposites. If we did not feel sorrow then how could we feel joy? If we did not feel love then we could not feel grief. If we have not been in the darkness then how could we appreciate the light? The extent to which we experience one is in direct proportion to the extent to which we experience its opposite.

I have become a more tolerant, less judgemental person. We are all on the same journey. Why not help each other along the way? I realise that everyone carries a secret pain that has moulded them into the person they have become.

I recognise the brevity and fragility of life and appreciate and value each moment. Life can be snatched from us at any moment without warning.

Knowing that I am not in control and trusting in a greater power has given me a tremendous freedom to enjoy each moment to the full. Nothing will ever be taken for granted again. Life is a gift to be lived gently, to be appreciated and savoured. Simply living life consciously is a prayer.

I wake up each morning with a sense of gratitude knowing that whatever the day may bring I will be able to cope with it, because I have been through the very worst and I have survived.

Our family has woven a rich, colourful life tapestry and Ciara has been an intricate, precious thread within it. But now that her thread is missing, we have been forced to begin a new tapestry. It is strong yet delicate. And it is simple: grief has taught us to discard complicated patterns. It is an open weave; every thread of it is visible.

It has a subtle beauty that only suffering can bring.

We do not strive in our weaving but rather let it unfold in the way that seems right at the time.

We are happy and contented with what we are weaving right now but our original tapestry is never far away. It is always on hand to be taken out and lovingly gazed upon.

Life can only be understood backwards,
but it must be lived forwards.

SOREN KIERKEGAARD

WHEN I LOOK BACK ON the time since Ciara's death, I now regard it as a sacred time. The concentrated effort required to get through each day focused my attention like nothing else could, on the question of evil and suffering in this world and their relationship to God. When I came to the realisation that no amount of theologising or rationalising could ever explain or justify the senseless murder of Ciara or the untold suffering of humanity, the sheer incomprehensibility of it all forced me to cry out to God in anguished hope that there would be an answer, and to sit and wait in the darkness.

This took some time until eventually a fissure opened that allowed me to penetrate that deep place within connecting me to God, the essence of everything. This in turn sharpened my senses in a way I had not experienced before. Never had I felt so much pain, yet never had I felt so much joy in the simple pleasures of life. Never had I felt so dead inside, yet never had I felt so alive to the external world around me. Never had I felt God so present in my life and so mysteriously a part of what I was experiencing. This allowed me to see this earthly segment of our life as a tiny part of a far greater eternity. From that perspective life took on a different emphasis, a different meaning. A shift had occurred and I was finally able to accept Ciara's death. The stranglehold of grief loosened and, like a butterfly emerging from its cocoon, I emerged a different person, with a different perspective on life.

This does not mean that I do not continue to long for Ciara's physical presence. I still grieve for her. I miss her acutely. I think of her every day, sometimes every moment of every day. There will always be a place in my heart that only she can fill and I treasure the twenty-seven years during which I enjoyed her vibrant, loving presence.

Ciara has gone now. Someday I too will die. Until then I want to live a peaceful, joyful and helpful life in the deep awareness of God's immanent presence.

I WISH TO THANK ALL those who helped me in so many different ways since the murder of Ciara. You are too numerous to name but you know who you are. A mere thanks does not seem adequate for the contribution you have made to my life.

I thank Denis, my husband and *anam chara*, our daughter Denise, her husband Ian and our four grandchildren, Ailish, Toby, Liam and Angus. You will never know how precious you all are to me.

First published in 2010 by
UWA Publishing
Crawley, Western Australia 6009
www.uwap.uwa.edu.au

THE UNIVERSITY OF
WESTERN AUSTRALIA
Achieving International Excellence

Grateful acknowledgement is made to the following for permission to print excerpts from *Benedictus* by John O'Donohue, published by Bantam Press, reprinted by permission of The Random House Group Ltd and *Collected Poems of W.H. Auden 1991*, edited by Edward Mendelson, published by Faber & Faber.

Every effort has been made to trace and acknowledge copyright material in this publication. The author and publisher would welcome information from copyright holders who could not be traced. Enquiries should be made to the publisher.

A full CIP record for this book is available from the National Library of Australia

ISBN 978-1-921401-64-0

Illustrations by Tracy Graffin

Typeset in 11 pt Adobe Garamond Pro

Printed and bound in Malaysia for Imago